# Mind Workout for
# Gifted Kids
## Puzzle book

**COLLINS & BROWN**

First published in Great Britain in 2005 by Collins & Brown Ltd

The Chrysalis Building,

Bramley Road,

London W10 6SP

An imprint of **Chrysalis** Books Group plc

Editor: Victoria Alers-Hankey

Design: Clare Barber


This book has been completed with the help of others with whom we are
exeptionally grateful.


10 9 8 7 6 5 4 3 2 1

British Library Cataloguing-in-Publication Data:

A catalogue record for this book is available from the British Library.


ISBN 1 84340 284 X

Colour reproduction by Anorax Imaging Ltd

Printed and bound by CT Printing, China

# contents

# The workout

## WHAT GOOD ARE PUZZLES?

Some people just love puzzles and others just can't see the point in them. The most common objection is that puzzles are not 'real' problems. People think they are just a pastime for anoraks. But puzzles do help to teach you to think. They are quite different from the sort of problems that you find in school books. A school book problem tells you exactly what result you are expected to find and even how you should find it; a puzzle will often hide that information from you. A favourite puzzle punch line is something like: 'Replace the question mark with a number'. This leaves you a huge amount of latitude and can make even the most mundane calculation into an intellectual adventure. Imagine trying to find your way around in a forest without way marks to guide you. The forest wouldn't have to be very big for you to get totally lost. This is pretty much what puzzles are like. If you are to succeed with them you must stay wide awake to all the possibilities and keep your thinking as flexible as possible. Don't assume that just because you saw a puzzle like this before the new one will be solved in the same way as the old one. Puzzles are tricky. They are deliberately constructed to mislead and mystify. But after a while you'll start to see how the setter's mind is working and you'll find yourself engaged in an intriguing battle of wits.

The puzzles in this book are not intended to be an IQ test. They have two purposes, first, to challenge you to use your intelligence in unusual ways and, second, to allow you to discover the sorts of mental activity you excel at and find most enjoyable. The puzzles are accessible to kids of a wide age span. They require very little previous knowledge. For example, any calculations required can be done with a little simple arithmetic and are quite easy enough to be completed by quite young children. But that – as you will soon discover – doesn't mean the puzzles themselves are easy.

## ESSENTIAL TOOLS

Before you start you must understand some of the ways in which puzzles work. First, we often use alphanumeric values. This may sound hard but all it means is that letters can be represented by numbers based on their position in the alphabet. To make things more interesting we can number the alphabet both forwards and backwards. If you don't know all the values by heart use the diagram below. A trick used by puzzle setters is to write the alphabet as a circle. This way if you have a puzzle that requires you to use, say, start at M and use every third letter, you don't stop at Z but keep on counting.

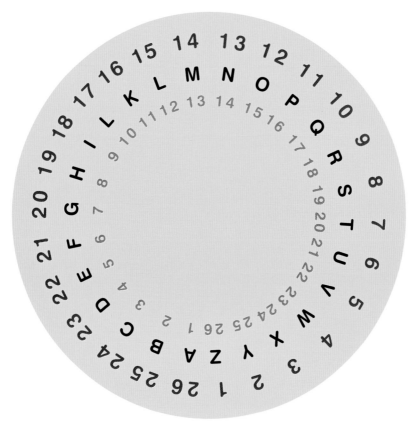

# 1. Test your general knowledge

## ① MATCH THE WORDS

Each of the words in the list below belongs logically to one of the lists at the bottom. Decide where each word must go.

**TRANQUIL**

**DRACULA**

**HOT**

**COUNTRY**

**THYME**

| A | B | C | D | E |
|---|---|---|---|---|
| MUMMY | HUMID | PEACEFUL | REALM | SAGE |
| WEREWOLF | WARM | QUIET | STATE | OREGANO |
| MONSTER | CLOSE | CALM | KINGDOM | BASIL |
| FRANKENSTEIN | SWEATY | RELAXED | REPUBLIC | CHIVES |
| DEMON | SUNNY | HAPPY | LAND | FENNEL |

## ② FAMILY PARTY

A family party consists of father, mother, son, daughter, brother, sister, cousin, nephew, niece, uncle, and aunt. Only two men and two women are present. They share an ancestor. Who are they?

## ③ COIN IN A BOTTLE

A small coin is pushed into a bottle and a cork pushed firmly into the open neck. Your task is to work out how to remove the coin without pulling the cork out or breaking the bottle.

## ④ RIDDLE

The Victorians were very fond of puzzles and especially riddles. See if you can find the answer to this one.

A VESSEL HAVE I,
THAT IS ROUND AS A PEAR,
MOIST IN THE MIDDLE,
SURROUNDED BY HAIR,
AND OFT TIMES IT HAPPENS,
THAT WATER FLOWS THERE

## ⑤ A WONDERFUL PUZZLE

The letters below may look mysterious but they represent things that you have probably heard of. You are unlikely to have seen more than one of these things because most of them ceased to exist long ago. Can you work out what they are? If you can name all of them without using an encyclopaedia you can give yourself an extra pat on the back.

GP @ G

HG of B

P @ A

S of Z @ O

C of R

T of A @ E

M @ H

## ⑥ A PROBLEM OF PLACES

These places may be unfamiliar but they have one thing in common. Can you discover what it is?

LUANDA

ASMARA

PORT AU PRINCE

JAKARTA

VIENTIANE

RABAT

TAIPEI

OUAGADOUGOU

TASHKENT

## ⑦ WHAT CAN YOU MAKE OF IT?

Below are ten names of well known stories that have been severely abbreviated. Can you work out what they mean?

THE HB OF N

SN & AND THE SD

THE C IN THE R

TK A M

A T OF TC

A IN W

C AND THE CF

THE A OF HF

THE L THE W AND THE W

THE LH ON THE P

## ⑧ A FAMILY AFFAIR

A family of seven people held a reunion every year.

The family consisted of: 2 mothers, 1 grandmother, 2 daughters, 2 sisters, 1 mother-in-law, 1 daughter-in-law, 2 fathers, 2 sons, 1 brother, 1 father-in-law, 3 grand-children, four children.

Can you explain how the people were related?

# 2. Letters and Words

## 1 GRID GAME

If you look closely at the grid you'll see that there is logic to the way it has been constructed. When you understand the logic you will be able to complete the grid.

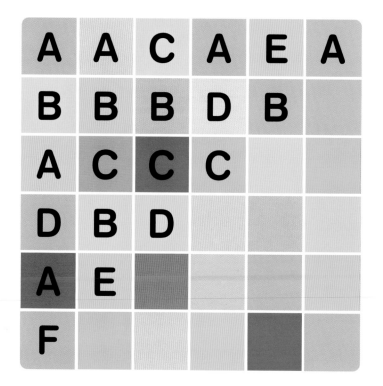

## 2 HIDDEN CONNECTION

These words have one thing in common. Can you find out what it is?

| | |
|---|---|
| VACATE | PIRATE |
| DOGGEREL | EPIGRAM |
| ATHENS | ANTHEM |
| MOSCOW | DEBUGGED |
| MAGNATE | ASSASSIN |

## 3 PERPLEXING PRESIDENTS

You can find four former US presidents concealed in the grid below. The way to find them is to take one letter from each column.

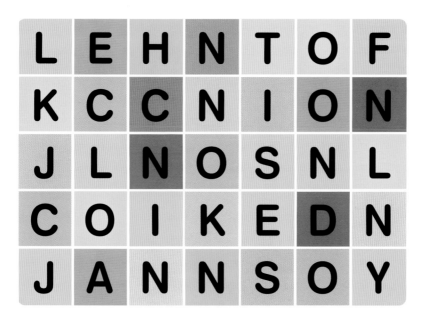

## ④ HIDDEN HOUNDS

Six dogs (**ROVER, FIDO, REX, BOUNCER, SPOT, and PATCH**) are hiding in the grid below. They have used a cunning trick to disguise their whereabouts. Can you find them?

| S | A | E | V | S | B | T | D | N | G |
|---|---|---|---|---|---|---|---|---|---|
| P | V | E | N | F | L | T | Q | P | U |
| W | S | O | Q | Y | M | B | N | V | S |
| F | O | L | A | E | N | C | T | Q | D |
| S | N | J | S | F | Y | P | V | B | T |
| X | A | L | T | M | R | V | O | U | O |
| B | G | J | E | P | F | O | L | D | E |
| H | B | E | V | A | O | D | I | I | A |
| A | I | N | G | D | Q | F | A | B | C |
| S | E | Y | N | T | A | S | C | N | Q |

## 5 WHAT'S THE CONNECTION?

The words below have something in common. Can you work out what it is and then find another word that could join the list?

SAIL
WANDER
TEAK
SILO
WILES
AURAL

## 6 ODD MAN OUT?

Here are some famous people. Who is the odd one out?

N A I L E B E T R S T N E I

N I O S T A W A E C N

Y J D F O E H N N K E N

G S N T I E K P H W E A N H

## 7 AIRPORT QUEST

Hidden in the grid below you will find the names of 9 international airports. The names can be found by moving from square to touching square. Many of the letters in the grid are dummies put there to confuse you. Can you find the right path and uncover all nine names?

| M | G | U | R | I | O | N | T | N | D |
| E | N | N | O | N | O | H | A | E | P |
| D | E | N | R | L | Y | H | R | G | M |
| I | B | A | O | A | R | E | E | E | O |
| O | E | H | A | L | N | A | J | L | B |
| Q | M | L | S | C | A | T | A | V | I |
| P | E | L | W | O | R | H | C | O | J |
| L | S | I | V | N | O | S | K | U | A |
| B | T | A | P | I | F | B | T | S | W |
| I | R | V | X | A | R | M | N | A | T |

# 8 SWEEPING UP

Congratulations! You have a vacation job. The bad news is that it's sweeping up after a party. On the floor you find the torn up name tags of the guests. A short inspection tells you that they were famous actors. Can you find the names of all the guests?

BRA   IAZ   H

ERRY

INA   TT

AN   D PI

CAME

RON D   K NO

ALLY B

LIE   RTER

ENA B   DY A

CA

WIN   NIC

LTE   HAM

K

GEL   ON

JO

SLET   LL EN

HEL   WOO

ATE

## ⑨ LETTERS FOR LUNCH?

If you examine the letters below carefully you'll see that there is something odd about them. This should lead you to the name of a German city associated with food.

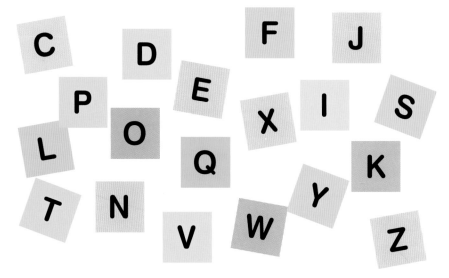

## ⑩ WHERE DOES IT GO?

The two lists of words have something in common. If you wanted to add the word **PHILOSOPHIES** would it go in the first column, the second column, or both?

| | |
|---|---|
| PRIMARY | TOKEN |
| DILEMMA | UPHILL |
| ANNEXE | FLEET |
| COCKATEELS | CONTRIVANCE |
| ANGINA | SESAME |

# 11 FAMOUS NAMES

Here's a gathering that contains dozens of the most famous people in the world, past and present. They are all VIPs so they don't want to be kept waiting. Your job is to get them seated in the grid as quickly as possible.

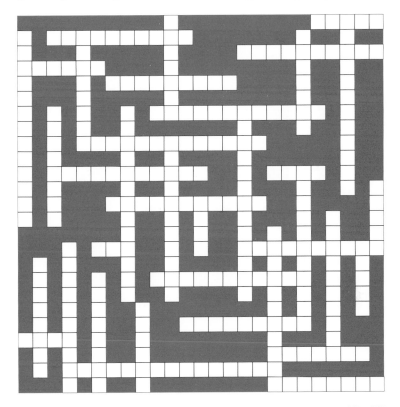

| | | | |
|---|---|---|---|
| ANGELINA JOLIE | CLINT EASTWOOD | JODIE FOSTER | SEAN CONNERY |
| ASHLEY OLSON | DAVID BOWIE | KATE MOSS | THE WIZARD OF OZ |
| ATTILA | ELTON JOHN | LENIN | RASPUTIN |
| BART SIMPSON | ELVIS | MICK JAGGER | ROBIN HOOD |
| BEYONCE | GABRIEL | MAO | SANTA CLAUS |
| BONO | GANDHI | MOSES | TROTSKY |
| BUFFALO BILL | GEORGE CUSTER | NERO | WOODY ALLEN |
| CALIGULA | GOLDILOCKS | NOAH | |
| CAMERON DIAZ | IVAN THE TERRIBLE | NOSTRADAMUS | |
| CHARLES DARWIN | JOAN BAEZ | PETER PAN | |

# ⑫ PRESIDENT PROBLEM

Below you'll find a list of American presidents arranged in alphabetical order. Your job is to fit them into the grid as quickly as possible.

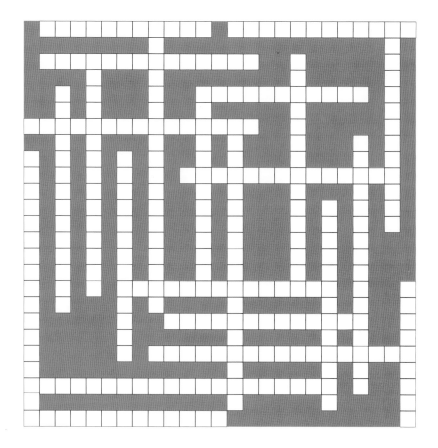

| JAMES BUCHANAN | WILLIAM HENRY HARRISON | FRANKLIN D ROOSEVELT |
| WILLIAM CLINTON | ANDREW JACKSON | WILLIAM HOWARD TAFT |
| GROVER CLEVELAND | THOMAS JEFFERSON | HARRY S TRUMAN |
| CALVIN COOLIDGE | ANDREW JOHNSON | JOHN TYLER |
| DWIGHT D EISENHOWER | ABRAHAM LINCOLN | MARTIN VAN BUREN |
| MILLARD FILLMORE | JAMES MONROE | GEORGE WASHINGTON |
| GERALD R FORD | RICHARD M NIXON | WOODROW WILSON |
| ULYSSES S GRANT | RONALD WILSON REAGAN | |

# 13 THE NAME GAME

All the names below can be fitted into the crossword grid. Your task is to see how quickly you can finish the job.

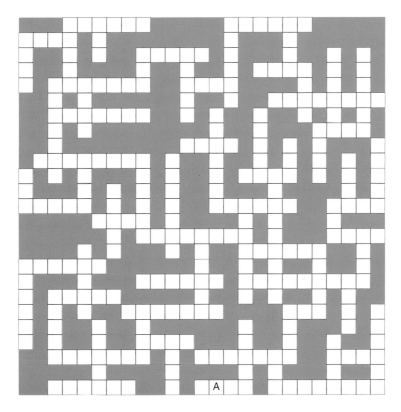

| ALEX | CRAIG | GORDON | JOHN | MARGARET | OTTO | SYLVIA |
|---|---|---|---|---|---|---|
| ANGELA | DAVID | GRAHAM | JUNE | MARIE | REX | TERRY |
| APRIL | DEREK | HELEN | KATE | MARY | ROBERT | TINA |
| BETSY | ELIZABETH | HILARY | KEITH | MAY | SAFFRON | TOM |
| BEN | FELICITY | HOLLY | KEVIN | MICKEY | SEAN | TRICIA |
| BRAD | FRANCIS | INGE | KURT | MIKE | SIOBHAN | RICHARD |
| CARL | FRED | JANE | KYLE | NELL | SID | WOLFGANG |
| CATHERINE | GABY | JANICE | LEE | NICK | SION | |
| CHARITY | GEORGIE | JEAN | LESLEY | ODETTE | SOPHIE | |
| CHARLES | GILLIAN | JEANNE | LILY | OLGA | STEFI | |
| COLIN | GLENYS | JIM | MALCOM | OMAR | SUSAN | |

---

# 3. Code Breakers

## ① SYMBOL SOLUTION

If this '👍✌🏳🖐❄✌☹  👍🖐❄✌👉💧'
spells 'capital cities',

try to work out the cities below.

# 2 CARD CODE

The cards below conceal a coded message. Can you discover how the code works and read the message?

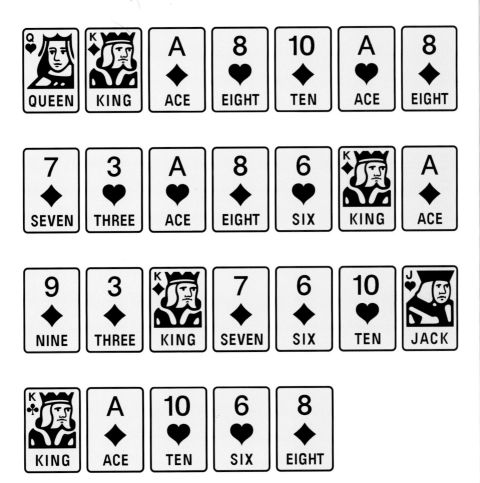

Row 1: QUEEN · KING · ACE · EIGHT · TEN · ACE · EIGHT

Row 2: SEVEN · THREE · ACE · EIGHT · SIX · KING · ACE

Row 3: NINE · THREE · KING · SEVEN · SIX · TEN · JACK

Row 4: KING · ACE · TEN · SIX · EIGHT

## ③ CODE CRACKER

| 1 | 9 | 8 | 6 | 6 | 5 | 7 | 4 | 10 | 10 | 8 | 7 | 3 |
|---|---|---|---|---|---|---|---|----|----|---|---|---|
| - | - | - | - | - | - | - | - | -  | -  | - | - | - |

| 4 | 1 | 10 | 4 | 3 | 9 | 10 | 78 | 7 | 8 | 10 | 10 |
|---|---|----|---|---|---|----|----|---|---|----|----|
| - | - | -  | - | - | - | -  | -  | - | - | -  | -  |

The above message is coded. It uses a logical sequence but each number represents two letters of the alphabet. Can you work out what it says?

## ④ TRIANGLE TRIBULATION

The number in the middle of each triangle is related to the letters at its points. The same relationship applies to all four triangles; what number should go in the last triangle?

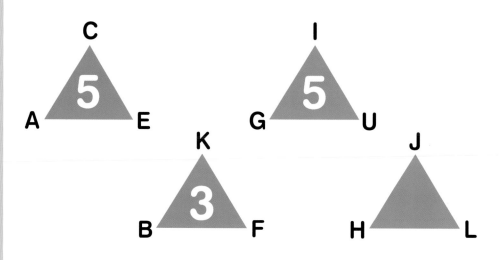

# 4. Series Fun

## ① STRANGE SEQUENCES

The following letters and numbers are all in series. Your job is to find out how each series works and what letter or number should be used to continue it. The first few are easy ones to get you started but to solve them all you'll need to rack your brains.

1.  M   T   W   T   F   S   ?

2.  O   T   T   F   F   S   S   E   N   ?

3.  M   V   E   M   J   S   U   N   ?

4.  T   F   S   E   T   T   F   ?

5.  N   W   H   O   I   I   E   I   I   ?

6.  D   N   O   S   A   J   J   M   A      ?

7.  R   O   Y   G   B   I   ?

8.  1   3   5   7   8   9   ?

9.  A   T   G   C   L   V   L   S   S   C   A   ?

10. R   K   B   K   Q   B   K   ?

## 2 A TRICKY PROBLEM

Take a look at this series:

It is actually something very familiar that you think about every day. However, we have not shown you the initial letter of each word and though they are presented in a logical order it is not the one you are used to. Can you work out what the series is and how it has been disguised?

## 3 A TRICKY PROBLEM

Look at the series below. Can you decide what the next letter should be and whether it should go above or below the line? You need to ask yourself two questions. First, what do the letters stand for and, second, what is the logic behind the division. As with all the puzzles the answer is simple but arriving at it may take you some time.

Y  H  Y  Y  T  R

---

Y  L  E  R  R

## ④ MORE STRANGE SERIES

In all these problems your task is the same – to discover the logic that the series is based on so that you can replace the questionmark with the correct letter or number.

1.  A   B   D   P   Q   ?

2.  100   365   24   60?

3.  6   6   7   9   8   6   ?

4.  A   H   I   M   O   ?

5.  1   1   2   3   5   8   13   21

6.  1   4   9   16   25 ?

7.  3   3   5   4   4   3   5   5   4   ?

8.  7   8   5   5   3   4   4   6   9   7   8   8   ?

9.  F   S   T   F   F   S   S   E   N ?

10. This one is a little bit different. From what he says can you discover Adam's surname?

'GOOD DAY, MADAM, I'M ADAM.'

# 5. Number Fun

## 1 ADD THE LETTERS

Here is an odd addition sum:

```
      E  E
  +  E  E  O
  ─────────────
  O  E  O  O
```

Each letter O represents an odd number and each letter E stands for an even number. Each digit from 0 to 9 has been used just once in the sum. (N.B Zero is an even number.) What should the sum look like?

## 2 FIND THE RULE

The pairs of numbers below are all related by the same simple rule. When you discover what it is you should be able to replace the question mark with a number.

| | |
|---|---|
| 3 | 15 |
| 2 | 11 |
| 7 | 31 |
| 5 | 23 |
| 6 | ? |

# 3 A STATE OF CONFUSION

Complete the grid with the letters of the word IDAHO. When completed no row, column or diagonal line will contain the same letters more than once. One horizontal line will spell the word correctly.

# 4 MASS MEETING

If ten people meet and all shake hands with each other, how many handshakes will there be all together?

## 5 TIME TEASER

This digital watch behaves in a very strange manner. It is, however, consistent so that once you discover what it is doing you should be able to predict what it will do next.

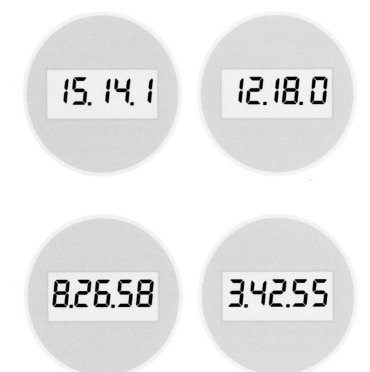

## 6 MAKING A ROUND HUNDRED

In this game you can use the nine digits only once each and always in their correct numerical order. You may multiply, add or subtract but the answer each time must be 100. How many ways to do this can you find?

# 7 FIND ME A NUMBER

This puzzle comes in two parts. Here's the first:

Make a number that uses some of the digits from 1 – 9 once only. You can use as many or as few as you like. However, when you have made your number you have to be able to put together the remaining digits to make another number that is double the first one.

Your second task is easier.
Find a way to write 1 using all the digits from zero to 9.

# 8 THE VERY MAGICAL SQUARE

Take the following numbers:

**8188    8111    1118    1888    8881    8118    8181    1188
8888    1111    1818    8811    8818    1811    1181    1881**

Now arrange them so that they make a magic square. The total of every row, column and diagonal must be 19,998.

You'll find that this square has even more remarkable properties than other magic squares. The four corners also add up to the same total. The square also works upside down (because 1 and 8 look the same upside down). It even continues to work if you view it in a mirror.

## 9 CUBE CONUNDRUM

The diagram shows four views of the same cube. What is opposite the blank face of the fourth cube?

## 10 ONE-WAY STREET

Technically problems like this are called unicursal puzzles. What you have to do is work out a way to reproduce the figure given without lifting your pencil from the paper or going over any line more than once.

# 11 FIND THE NUMBERS

Work out the logic of this grid and you will be able to replace the question marks with numbers.

| A | B | C | D | E |
|---|---|---|---|---|
| 3 | 2 | 5 | 10 | 5 |
| 7 | 1 | 8 | 14 | 6 |
| 9 | 4 | 13 | 15 | 2 |
| 11 | 1 | ? | 13 | ? |

## 12 COLUMN CALCULATIONS

In the grid below the columns are related to each other by a simple formula.

Can you discover what it is and replace the question marks with numbers?

| A | B | C | D | E |
|---|---|---|---|---|
| 7 | 4 | 4 | 16 | 3 |
| 9 | 5 | 2 | 4 | 4 |
| 12 | 6 | 5 | ? | 6 |
| 13 | 4 | 6 | 36 | 9 |
| 6 | 2 | 3 | 9 | ? |

## 13 FAMILY PARTY

| Q | R | ÷ | S | X | T | = | U | | V |
|---|---|---|---|---|---|---|---|---|---|
| - | | | - | | + | | | | ÷ |
| W | X | + | Y | - | U | = | R | | V |
| | | | | | - | | | | |
| T | U | ÷ | Z | ÷ | S | = | R | | |

The numbers in this sum have been replaced by letters. All of the numbers from 0 to 9 have been used and by telling you that R = 2 we hope to give you enough information to make only one solution possible. Each letter represents the same number as pften as it appears. Can you work out the original sum?

## 14 GETTING TO THE ROOT OF THE PROBLEM

The columns of figures have a logical connection. Find out what it is and replace the question mark with a number.

| 1089 | 576 | 57 |
|------|------|----|
| 961 | 484 | 53 |
| 361 | 1764 | ? |

## ⑮ KNIGHT NAMES

There four names (two boys and two girls) hidden in this grid. To find them you must go from letter to letter moving like a knight in chess (three squares straight and one to either side). If you find the right place to start all the names will be revealed.

| A | J | E | Y | L |
|---|---|---|---|---|
| T | G | L | E | P |
| O | T |   | E | M |
| R | O | O | N | C |
| R | H | A | M | N |

# 16 LONG DIVISION

Here's a long division sum showing all the working and leaving no remainder. Each of the numbers from 0 to 9 appears in the sum – the 'numbers' K, E & G appearing an apt number of times. Each letter stands for the same number as often as it appears. What is the sum?

```
            C D E F G
        ┌─────────────────
A B )  A D G A A H D
       A J K
       A K A
       A A G
           F A
           J F
           A G H
           A E E
               F D
```

# 6. Fun Workouts

## 1 PLACE THE LETTERS

Here are two columns of letters:

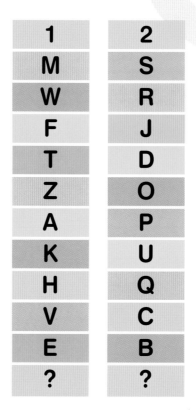

| 1 | 2 |
|---|---|
| M | S |
| W | R |
| F | J |
| T | D |
| Z | O |
| A | P |
| K | U |
| H | Q |
| V | C |
| E | B |
| ? | ? |

Which letters would you put in the bottom boxes? There are several possibilities for Column 1 but only one for Column 2.

## 2 MISSING VOWELS

Here are ten famous quotations from the same author. The vowels have been taken out and the words run together but punctuation has been left in to give you some clues. Can you unravel all of them?

1. TBRNTTB:THTSTHQSTN:

2. LL'SWLLTHTNDSWLL.

3. FRNDS,RMNS,CNTRYMN,LNDMYRRS;

4. WHNSHLLWTHRMTGN?

5. LLMTBYMNLGHT,PRDTTN.

6. NWSTHWNTRFRDSCNTNT

7. PLGNBTHYRHSS!

8. FMSCBTHFDFLVE,PLYN;

9. SWRNTBYTHMN,THNCNSTNTMN,

10. FREWLL!GDKNWSWHNWSHLLMTGN.

## 3 COLOUR CONUNDRUM

The colours below all have something in common, except for one. Can you spot which is the odd one out?

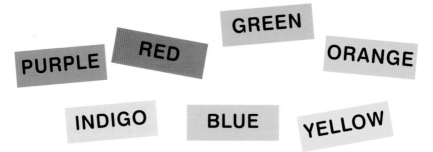

PURPLE   RED   GREEN   ORANGE

INDIGO   BLUE   YELLOW

## 4 DIAMOND MINE

Look carefully at the diagram. What should go in the blank section?

# 5 TILE TRAUMA

Four of your exquisite hand-made ceramic tiles have been destroyed by a clumsy family member. Of course you will repair the damage but can you work out which tiles you need to complete the pattern logically?

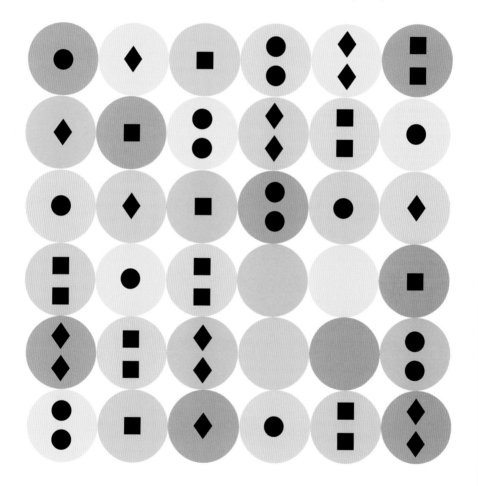

# 6 PATTERN PROBLEM

Using just two straight lines you must divide the square into three sections.

Each section must contain 4 dots, 5 diamonds, 4 spades, and 3 hearts.

# 7 JUST ANOTHER MISSING LETTER?

This is one of those occasions when it is important to keep alert if you want to solve the problem. Once you understand the logic of the puzzle you will be able to replace the question mark with a letter.

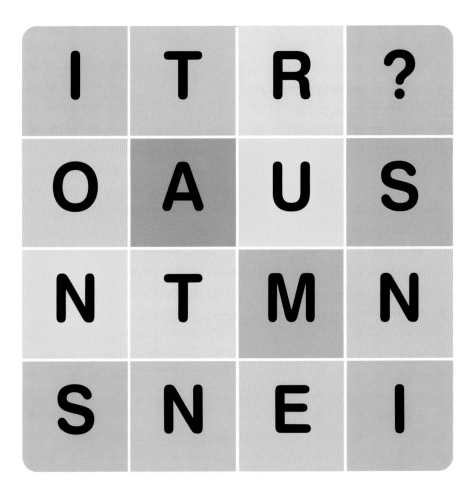

## ⑧ ODD ONE OUT

One of the grids below clearly doesn't fit with the others. Can you work out which one it is?

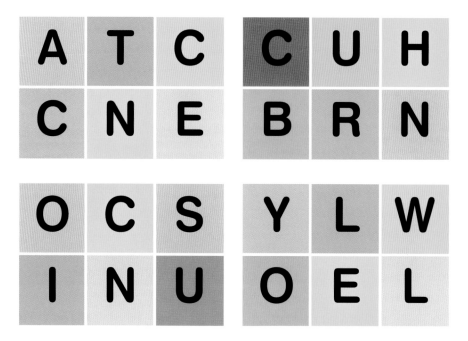

## 9 MIXED MESSAGE

The messages below may look as if it is the product of some highly complex coding system. In fact, if you look closely you should be able to read it with ease.

**CHDGANFERYNA**

**OOUBFGMKELAK**

**EAMDSENDENSE**

**LTYOHETFHEYT**

**HIEHISNEGMNE**

**RESSAGE**

## 10 COUNTING KINGS

### BEN 2

### KEVIN 5

### HARRY 6

### RICHARD 8

Above you'll see listed the kings of a strange foreign land. The name of each new king is chosen according to an ancient system. The number plays a crucial part in the choice of name. The next king will have the number 11. Can you find a name for him?

## ⑪ A VERY CLEVER PUZZLE?

Some puzzles are just too clever for their own good. This one was shown to a group of kids by a teacher who had spent some time constructing the puzzle but who got an answer that he wasn't expecting. Can you find two answers to the puzzle? What is the next letter in this series?

# C H L O ?

## ⑫ STRANGE SIGNPOST

This is an odd signpost. A moment's thought will tell you that the distances given can't be right. So what do the numbers mean? If you work it out you should be able to calculate the distance to Rome.

**PARIS 800**   **COPENHAGEN 1600**

**LONDON 1000**   **VIENNA 900**

**OSLO 600**

## 13 WHAT'S THE CONNECTION?

It's important in puzzles to keep an open mind. If you don't you may find that something really simple has escaped your notice. For example, the numbers below have something in common. By performing a very simple mathematical operation you will soon see the connection. But will you ever think of the right way to view the problem? That remains to be seen.

## 5330   9695   9590   9305   8875

## 14 LETTER LOGIC

The letters and numbers below are related. Once you know what the letters stand for you will quickly work out how we arrived at the numbers and will be able to replace the question mark.

## E6  A6  A9  A10  A4  N12  S?

# ⑮ MYSTERY NUMBER

Below you will see a list of letters some of which have numbers. All you have to do is work out what the letters represent and then replace the question mark with a number. To make the game a bit tougher we have not put the letters in their normal order. Try swapping them around until they remind you of something familiar.

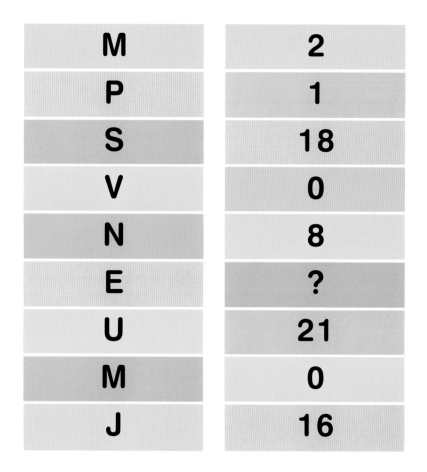

|  |  |
|---|---|
| M | 2 |
| P | 1 |
| S | 18 |
| V | 0 |
| N | 8 |
| E | ? |
| U | 21 |
| M | 0 |
| J | 16 |

## 16 LETTER LOGIC

As long as you have remembered what you read in the Introduction this puzzle should be very simple. Think about the relationships between the letters and you will soon work out what letter replaces the question mark.

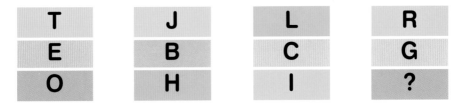

| T | J | L | R |
| E | B | C | G |
| O | H | I | ? |

## 17 MISSING LETTER MYSTERY

The square below follows a logical pattern. When you have worked out what it is you should be able to replace the question mark with a letter.

| J | K | M | F |
|---|---|---|---|
| S | E | B | N |
| Q | L | C | H |
| V | D | M | ? |

## 18 MAKING THE MOST OF IT

Start at A and make your way to B. You must move from square to touching square picking up numbers as you go. You may move only directly upwards or directly to the right on each move. What is the maximum score you can obtain?

**B**

| 56 | 65 | 19 | 25 | 65 |
|----|----|----|----|----|
| 34 | 20 | 9  | 6  | 19 |
| 9  | 6  | 9  | 20 | 65 |
| 34 | 20 | 9  | 6  | 9  |
| 19 | 25 | 46 | 56 | 65 |

**A**

## 19 SQUARE SUBTERFUGE

Is this just another square problem or is it something altogether different? Look carefully at the letters and see how they are related. You should be able to find the missing letter.

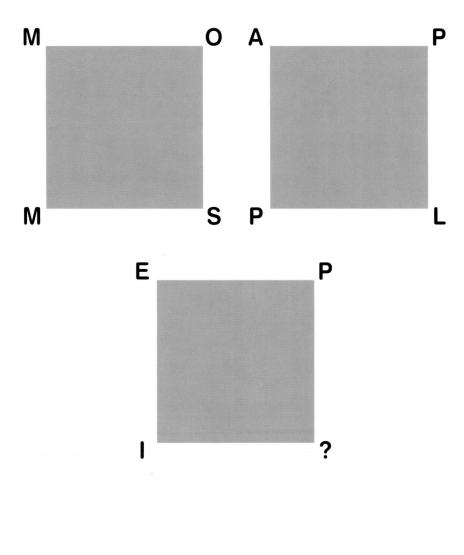

M     O    A     P

M     S    P     L

E     P

I     ?

# Solutions

## 1. TEST YOUR GENERAL KNOWLEDGE

**1** A – DRACULA. B – HOT. C – TRANQUIL. D – COUNTRY, E – THYME.

**2** They are a brother (with his son but without his wife) and a sister (without her husband but with her daughter).

**3** Push the cork right into the bottle and then tip the coin out.

**4** An eye.

**5** They are the seven wonders of the ancient world – the Great Pyramid at Giza, the Hanging Gardens of Babylon, the Pharos at Alexandria, the statue of Zeus at Olympia, the Colossus of Rhodes, the Temple of Artemis at Ephesus and the Mausoleum at Halicarnassus.

**6** They are the capital cities of the following countries – Angola, Eritrea, Haiti, Indonesia, Laos, Morocco, Taiwan, Burkina Faso, Uzbekistan

**7** The Hunchback of Notre Dame, Snow White and the Seven Dwarfs, The Catcher in the Rye, To Kill a Mockingbird, A Tale of Two Cities, Alice in Wonderland, Charlie and the Chocolate Factory, The Adventures of Huckleberry Finn, The Lion, the Witch and the Wardrobe, The Little House on the Prairie.

**8** There were 2 sisters and their brother, their mother and father, and their fathers' parents.

## 2. LETTERS AND WORDS

**1** The pattern works diagonally across the board from the top left. The series is A, AB, ABC, ABCD, ABCDE, ABCDEF. ⬇

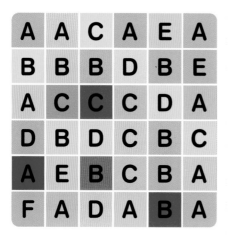

**2** They all contain the name of a creature – cat, dog, hen, cow, gnat, rat, pig, ant, bug, ass.

**3** KENNEDY, JOHNSON, CLINTON, JACKSON.

**4** The letters have all been moved one place in the alphabet so that A = B, B = C, C = D, etc. ⬇

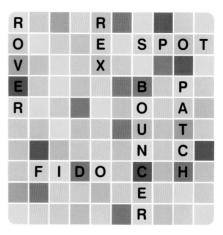

**5** All the words are anagrams of names (LISA, ANDREW, KATE, LOIS, LEWIS, LAURA).

**6** There are three scientists: Albert Einstein, Isaac Newton and Stephen Hawking. The odd one out is John F. Kennedy.

**7** ⬆ Larnaca, Orly, Heathrow, Shannon, O'Hare, Jacksonville, Ben Gurion, Tegel

**8** BRAD PITT, CAMERON DIAZ, HALLY BERRY, ANGELINA JOLIE, NICK NOLTE, HELENA BONHAM CARTER, KATE WINSLET, WOODY ALLEN

**9** The letters form an entire alphabet except for A B G H M R U which can be used to make the word HAMBURG.

**10** It could go in both. The first column contains girls' names (Mary, Emma, Anne, Kate, Gina and Sophie). The second column contains boys' names (Ken, Phil, Lee, Ivan, Sam).

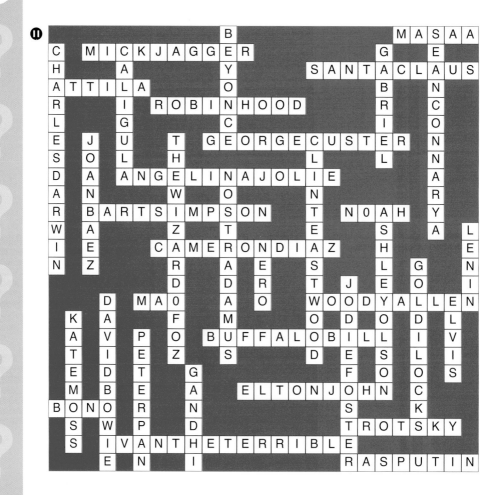

⑫

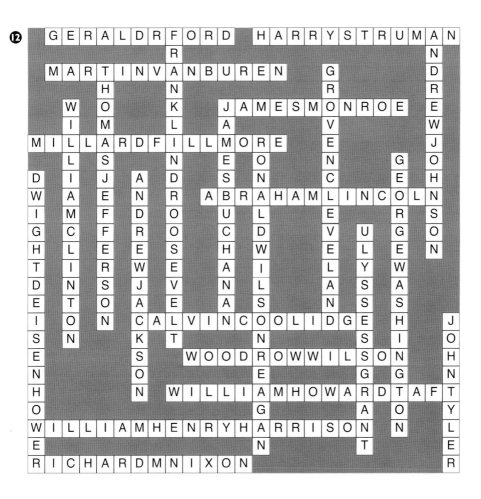

**58**

❸

```
      S Y L V I A                J A N I C E
K U R T     E       E                    E                    A                T   O
E       E   E       B E T S Y            A              N E L L        R   D
I       F   E               U                        I            I   E
T   S I O B H A N           S I O N      E        F E L I C I T Y
    A   M               A       E              Y      I   T
    F R A N C I S       N   C            A            I   T
    F   R                   C H          P        J A N E
    R                 S E A N   R        R        O            K
  W O L F G A N G     R       R          I   E    H   J        E
S   N   R       R     I       L   A L E X     N   U            V
I       E   H   A     C       E          L        N            I
D A V I D   E   H     H       S O P H I E        J E A N
        O L G A   A           A   Z              I
        E   M A R G A R E T   A          M I K E
    H   N       D   N     R O B E R T            Y
G O R D O N         G     I   E       E          L
L       L       L E S L E Y   C A T H E R I N E
E   C O L I N       L     K   H              R   I
N   R   Y   G I L L I A N         M A Y      C   H
Y   A   D   N           M         A          K   I
S   I   E   G A B Y     A         R          O   L
    G E O R G I E   R   C H A R I T Y        T I N A
    E           A       I   O                T   R
    M I C K E Y     D   K A T E   M A L C O M   Y
```

# 3. CODE BREAKERS

**❶** WASHINGTON  LONDON  BERLIN
CANBERRA  DUBLIN  WARSAW
BERLIN  SANTIAGO  BUDAPEST
MADRID

**❷** 'Congratulations, you've done it.' The
cards of the two suits were laid out in
the usual order. That gives 26 cards
and the 26 letters of the alphabet
were each allocated a card in order –
starting with the Ace of Hearts (the
King and so on).

**❸** 'A rolling stone gathers no moss.'
A/B = 1, C/D = 2, E/F = 3, etc)

**❹** The consonants are worth 1 and the
vowels 2. Add them all together and
put the sum in the centre.

# 4. SERIES FUN

**❶** **1.** The initial letters of the days of the
week.
**2.** The initial letters of the numbers
from 1 to 10.

**3.** The first letter of each word gives
you the first letter of the planets, in
order: Mercury, Venus, Earth, Mars,
Jupiter, Saturn, Uranus, Neptune,
Pluto.
**4.** These are the initial letters of the
even numbers 2–14
**5.** These are the second letter of each
number from 1–10
**6.** These are the initial letters of the
months December – March.
**7.** These are the initial letters of the
spectrum: Red, Orange, Yellow,
Green, Blue, Indigo, Violet.
**8.** These are the initial letters of the
numbers containing an E in their
name.
**9.** These the initial letters of the signs
of the zodiac. The missing one is
Pisces.
**10.** These are the initial letters of
chess pieces: Rook, Knight, Bishop,
King, Queen, Bishop, Knight, Rook.

**❷** First, we sorted the days of the week
into alphabetical order. Then we took
from each day the letter that comes
immediately before 'day'.

**❸ 1.** These are all the letters having an enclosed space.

**2.** 100 years in a century, 365 days in a year, 24 hours in a day, 60 minutes in an hour, & 60 seconds in a minute.

**3.** Beginning with Sunday, each number represents the number of letters in each day of the week.

**4.** These all letters that can be flipped horizontally and still remain the same. The rest would be T U V W X Y Z.

**5.** This is what is called a Fibonacci series. Each number is made by the addition of the two previous numbers.

**6.** These are square numbers. (1 x 1 = 1, 2 x 2 = 4, 3 x 3 = 9, etc.)

**7.** Each number is the number of letters in the word for each number from ONE to TEN.

**8.** Each number is the number of letters in each month of the year, starting with January.

**9.** These are the initial letters of First, Second, Third, etc.

**10.** The sentence is a palindrome (ie, it reads the same backwards as it does forwards). Adam's surname must be 'Good day' backwards which is Yaddoog.

## 5. NUMBER FUN

**❶** It could look like this:

$$
\begin{array}{r}
7\ 4\ 6 \\
2\ 8\ 9\ + \\
\hline
1\ 0\ 3\ 5
\end{array}
$$

**❷** The rule is n x 4+3.

**❸**

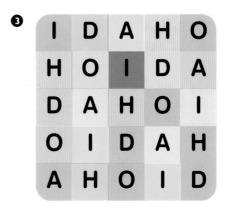

**❹** 45.

**❺** 21.14.51. Hours move back 3, 4, 5, and 6 hours. Minutes move on 4, 8, 16, and 32 minutes. Seconds move back 1, 2, 3, and 4.

**6** Here are some ways it can be done.
If you got more than this give yourself
a pat on the back.

123 − 4 − 5 − 6 − 7 + 8 − 9 = 100

12 + 3 − 4 + 5 + 67 + 8 + 9 = 100

(1 x 2) + 34 + 56 + 7 − 8 + 9 = 100

1 + (2 x 3) + 4 + 5 + 67 + 8 + 9 = 100

(1 + 2 − 3 − 4) (5 − 6 − 7 − 8 − 9) = 100

1 + (2 x 3) + (4 x 5) − 6 + 7 + (8 x 9) =100

- (1 x 2) − 3 − 4 − 5 + (6 x 7) + (8 x 0) = 100

1 + 2 + 3 + 4 + 5 + 6 + 7 + (8 x 9) = 100

**7** 6729 and 13458.

$$\frac{148}{296} + \frac{35}{70} = 1$$

**8**

| | | | |
|---|---|---|---|
| 8818 | 1111 | 8188 | 1881 |
| 8181 | 1888 | 8811 | 1118 |
| 1811 | 8881 | 1818 | 8111 |
| 8118 | 1188 | 8888 | 1181 |

**9**

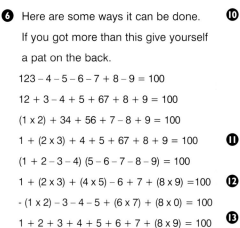

**10**

**11** 12 and 1. A + B = C. D − C = E.

**12** A − B = E, C2 = D. 4 and 25.

**13**

| 7 2 | / | 9 | x | 5 | = | 4 0 |
|---|---|---|---|---|---|---|
| - | | - | | + | = | / |
| 1 8 | + | 6 | - | 4 | = | 2 0 |
| 5 4 | / | 3 | / | 9 | = | 2 |

**14** Add the square roots of the first two
numbers to get the third.

**15** Follow the numbers and you get:
Tommy, Grace, John and Petronella.

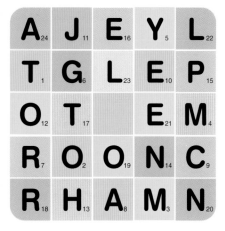

**⓰**

```
              8  6  3  7  4
   1  9 ) 1  6  4  1  1  0  6
          1  5  2
             1  2  1
             1  1  4
                7  1
                5  7
                1  4  0
                1  3  3
                   7  6
```

# 6. FUN WORKOUTS

**❶** All the letters in Column 1 are made of straight lines. All the letters in Column 2 have curves. The only letter with curves that has not been used is G.

**❷** 1. To be, or not to be: that is the question:

2. All's Well That Ends Well.

3. Friends, Roman countrymen lend me your ears;

4. When shall we three meet again?

5. Ill met by moonlight, proud Titania.

6. Now is the winter of our discontent

7. A plague on both your houses!

9. If music be the food of love, play on.

10. O! Swear not by the moon, the inconstant moon,

11. Farewell! God knows when we shall meet again.

**❸** INDIGO is the only colour with no E in it.

**❹** Two circles. (Look at every large diamond composed of four smaller ones; they each contain a black diamond in three of the sections and two circles in the other).

**❺**

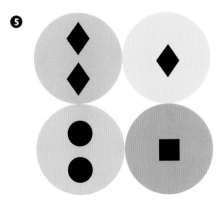

**6**

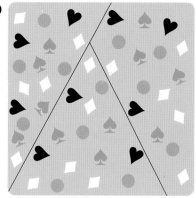

**7** The letters make the word 'instrumentations' spelled backwards. The first T is missing.

**8** Each grid contains an anagram. The first three, ACCENT, BRUNCH, and COUSIN are in alphabetical order. The last is YELLOW which does not continue the series.

**9** It says, 'Can you read this message?' The first letter of each word is succeeded by three random letters, then the rest of the word is given correctly and is followed by three more random letters.

**10** The number refers to the number of letters in the alphabet between the first and second letters of the name. Any name that has first and second letters 11 places apart will be accepted.

**11** The 'clever' answer is Q. The letters are 5, 4 , 3 and then 2 spaces apart in the alphabet. However, you may notice that if you put an E at the end you get CHLOE which is an answer that is every bit as sensible and much easier to spot.

**⑫** The numbers are based on the number of vowels and consonants in each name. A vowel is worth 100 and a consonant is worth 200. So:

Paris = 600 + 200 = 800
London = 800 + 200 = 1000
Copenhagen = 1200 + 400 = 1600
Vienna = 600 + 300 = 900
Oslo = 400 + 200 = 600
So Rome = 600

**⑬** If you divide the numbers by 5 you will get some important historical dates:
1066 (Battle of Hastings), 1939 (start of World War II), 1918 (start of World War 1), 1861 (start of American Civil War), 1775 (start of American War of Independence).

**⑭** The letters are the initial of the continents and the numbers are the number of letters in each name:
Europe 6, Africa 6, Australia 9, Antarctica10, Asia 4, North America12, South America 12.

**⑮** The letters stand for the planets of the solar system. The numbers are the number of moons that each planet has (we excluded any tiny objects). The missing one is Earth which, of course, has only one moon.

**⑯** Each grid contains a simple subtraction using alphanumeric values (see page 7). The answers are: 20 – 5 = 15, 10 – 2 = 8, 12 – 3 = 9, and 18 – 7 = 11. The eleventh letter is K.

**⑰** If you had the alphanumeric values of the letters in each row you get 40. To make this true of the bottom row you need A = 1

**⑱** 369. 19, 25, 46, 56, 65, 9, 65, 19, 65

**⑲** This is no mathematical formula. The letters spell, 'Mom's apple pie'.